MEL BAY'S HARMONICA HANDBOOK

by William Bay

1 2 3 4 5 6 7 8 9 0

PROPER POSITION

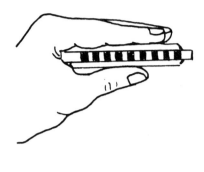

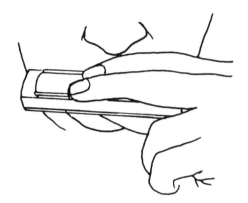

Left Hand   **Playing Position**

Vibrato Position

DIATONIC NOTE FINDER

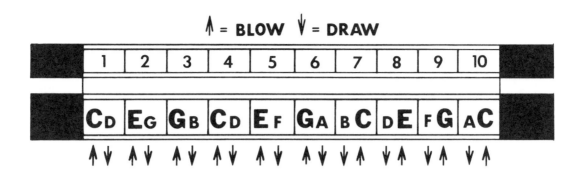

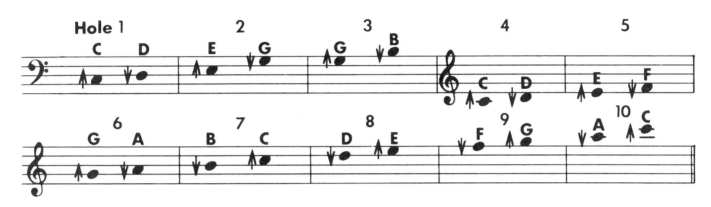

ON TOP OF OLD SMOKEY

↑ = Blow
↓ = Draw

Kentucky Mountain Song

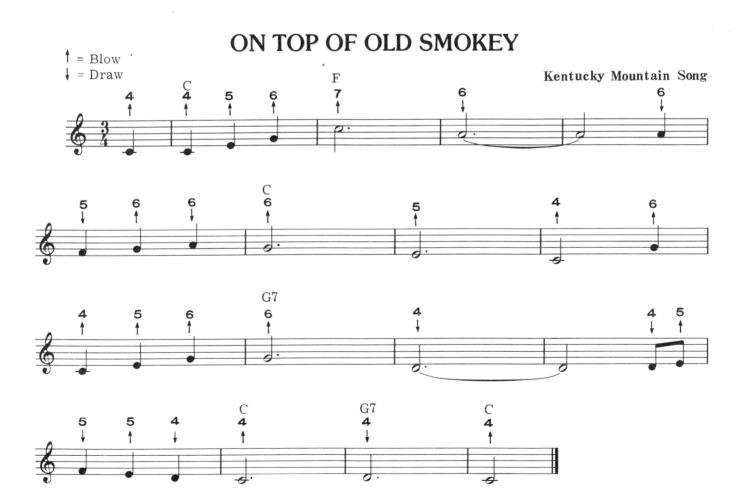

DIATONIC NOTE FINDER

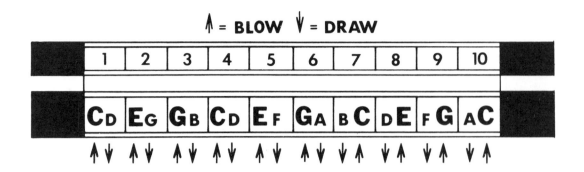

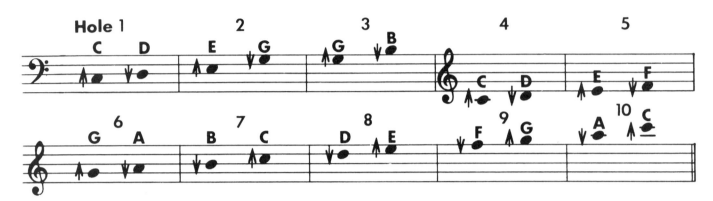

SWANEE RIVER

DIATONIC NOTE FINDER

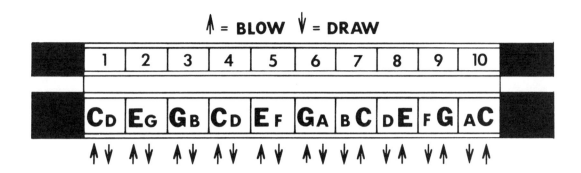

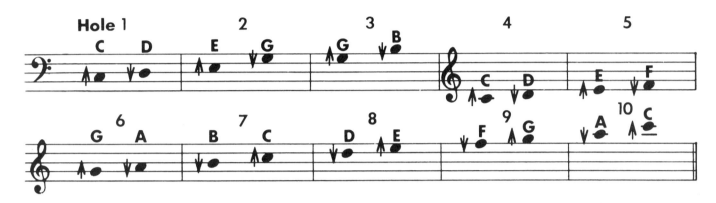

RED RIVER VALLEY

DIATONIC NOTE FINDER

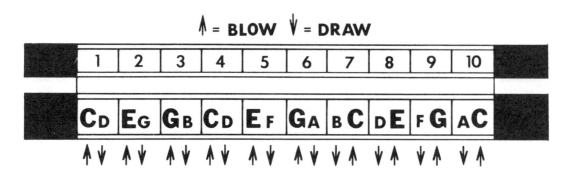

SHENANDOAH

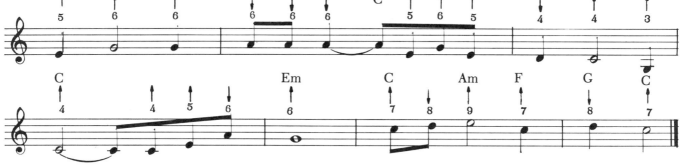

HOME ON THE RANGE

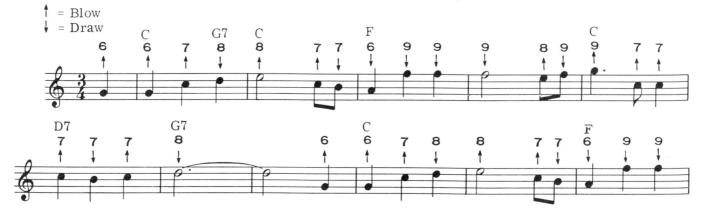

RESTS

A REST is a sign to designate a period of silence. This period of silence will be of the same duration as the note to which it corresponds.

𝄽 THIS IS A QUARTER REST

𝄾 THIS IS AN EIGHTH REST

𝄿 THIS IS A SIXTEENTH REST

━ THIS IS A HALF REST
Note that it lays on the line.

━ THIS IS A WHOLE REST
Note that it hangs down from the line.

NOTES

WHOLE 4 COUNTS	HALF 2 COUNTS	QUARTER 1 COUNT	EIGHTH 2 FOR 1 COUNT	SIXTEENTH 4 FOR 1 COUNT

RESTS

THE TIME SIGNATURE

The above examples are the common types of time signatures to be used in this book.

$\frac{4}{4}$ 4 beats per measure

a quarter-note receives one beat.

$\frac{4}{4}$ The top number indicates the number of beats per measure

The bottom number indicates the type of note receiving one beat beats per measure

$\frac{6}{8}$ **6** BEATS PER MEASURE

8 EACH EIGHTH-NOTE RECEIVES ONE FULL BEAT
(See p. 26 & 27)

Signifies so called "common time" and is simply another way of designating $\frac{4}{4}$ time.

DIATONIC NOTE CHART

↑ = BLOW ↓ = DRAW

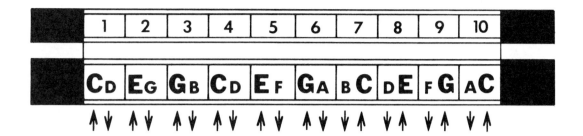

READING HARMONICA MUSIC

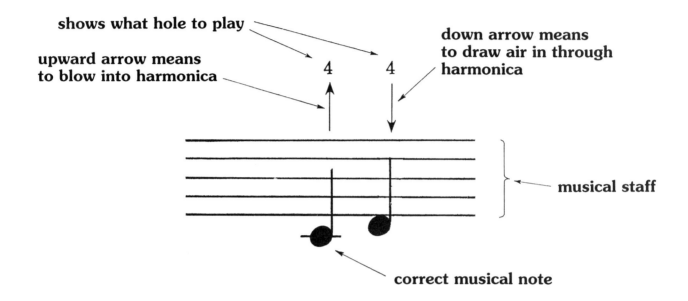

PLAYING ONLY ONE NOTE

(Tone Blocking)

There are two ways of blocking out undesired extra notes. One way is with the lips. With this technique the harp player simply purses his or her lips so that only one tone sounds. This method can restrict your technique a bit later on. The best and most difficult method is by "tongue blocking." With this method your tongue covers and blocks off the three undesired holes on the right. While this method takes a degree of patience to learn, it is preferable, especially for blues.

Tongue blocks 3 holes,
fourth hole sounds.

TYPES OF NOTES

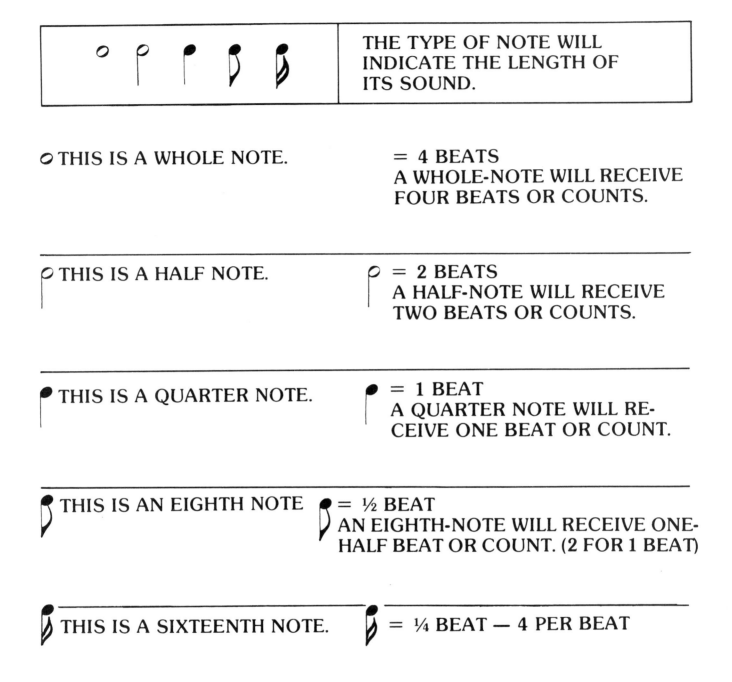

| | THE TYPE OF NOTE WILL INDICATE THE LENGTH OF ITS SOUND. |

THIS IS A WHOLE NOTE.

= 4 BEATS
A WHOLE-NOTE WILL RECEIVE FOUR BEATS OR COUNTS.

THIS IS A HALF NOTE.

= 2 BEATS
A HALF-NOTE WILL RECEIVE TWO BEATS OR COUNTS.

THIS IS A QUARTER NOTE.

= 1 BEAT
A QUARTER NOTE WILL RECEIVE ONE BEAT OR COUNT.

THIS IS AN EIGHTH NOTE

= ½ BEAT
AN EIGHTH-NOTE WILL RECEIVE ONE-HALF BEAT OR COUNT. (2 FOR 1 BEAT)

THIS IS A SIXTEENTH NOTE.

= ¼ BEAT — 4 PER BEAT

DIATONIC NOTE FINDER

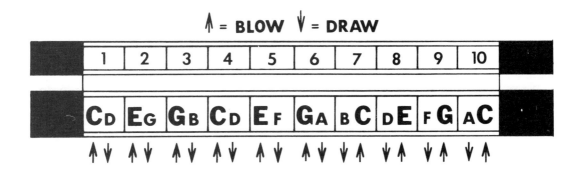

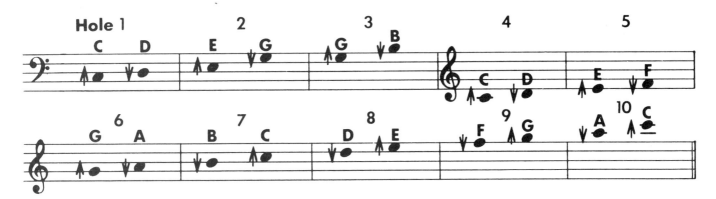

OH, SUSANNA

DIATONIC NOTE FINDER

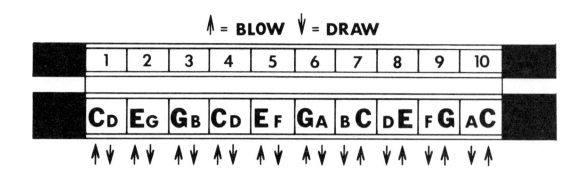

I'VE GOT PEACE LIKE A RIVER

DIATONIC NOTE FINDER

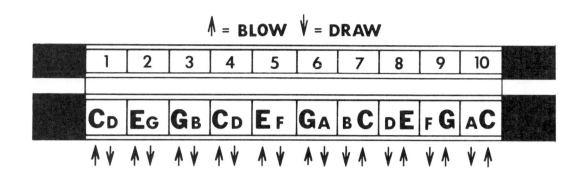

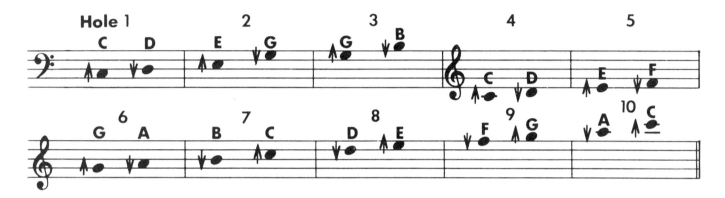

BLOW, YE WINDS

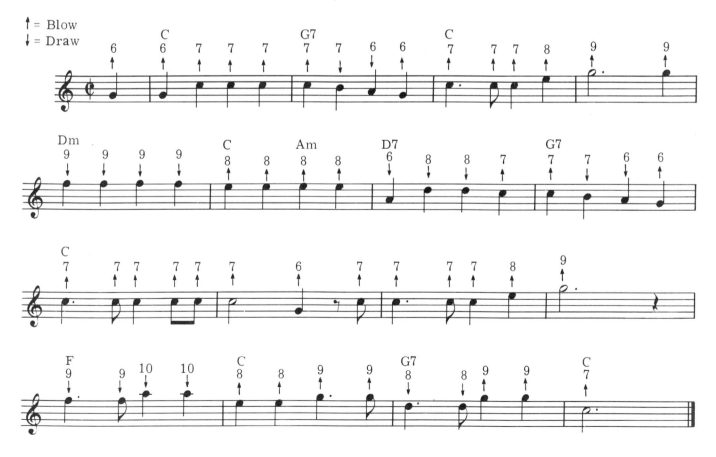

DIATONIC NOTE FINDER

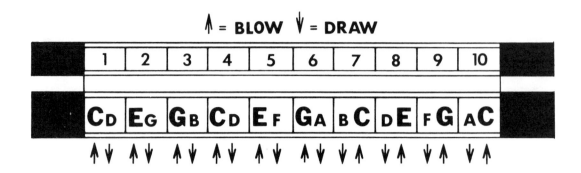

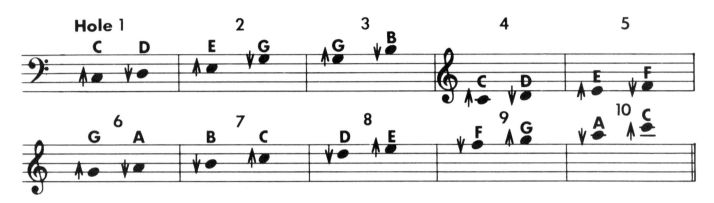

SWEET BETSY FROM PIKE

DIATONIC NOTE FINDER

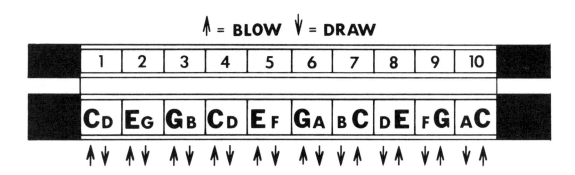

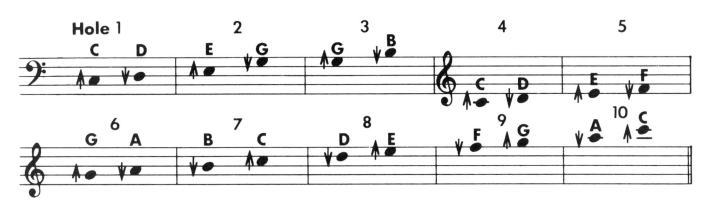

SHE WORE A YELLOW RIBBON

DIATONIC NOTE FINDER

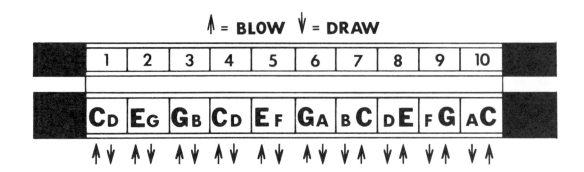

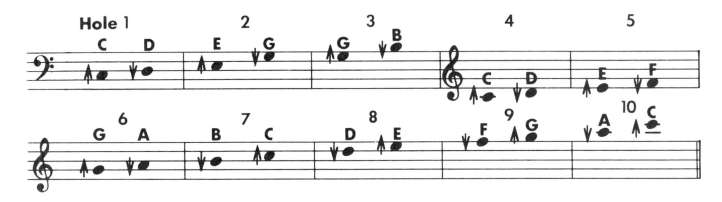

SANTA LUCIA

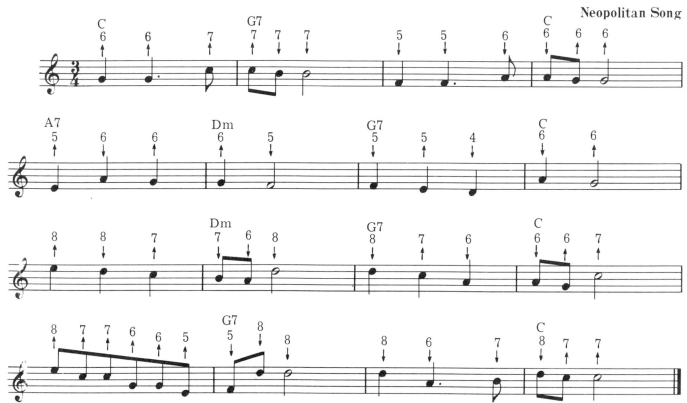

DIATONIC NOTE FINDER

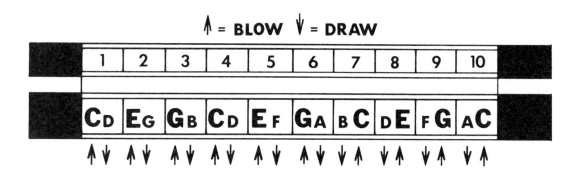

DUNDERBECK'S MACHINE

DIATONIC NOTE FINDER

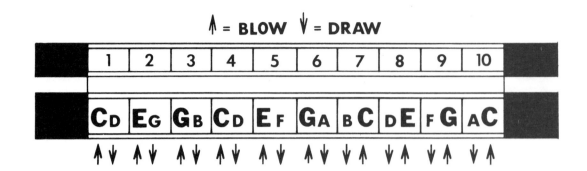

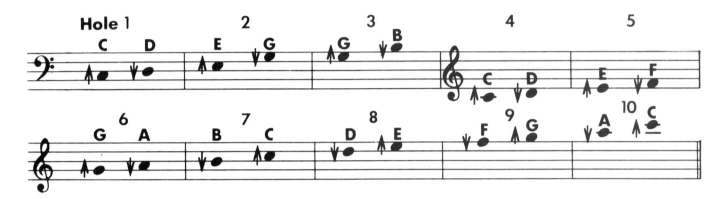

FAR ABOVE CAYUGA'S WATERS

16

DIATONIC NOTE FINDER

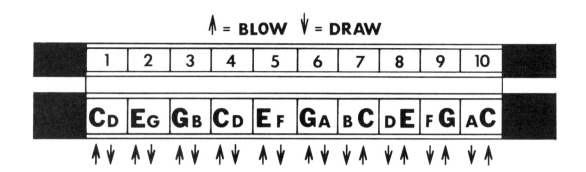

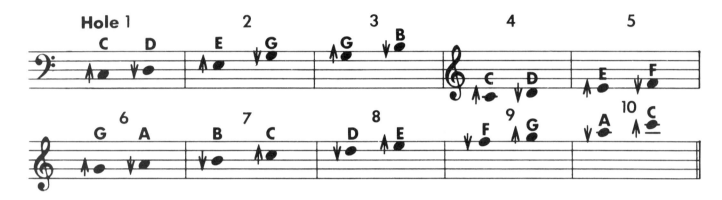

OUR BOYS WILL SHINE TONIGHT

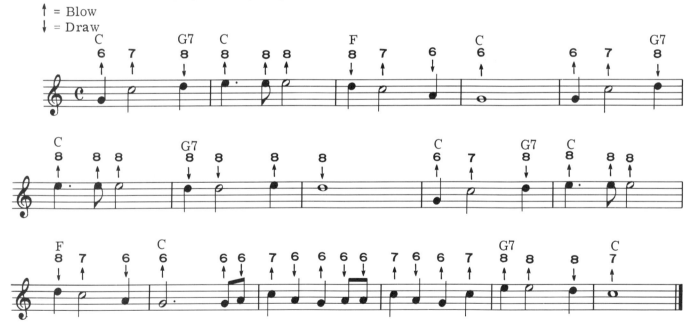

DIATONIC NOTE FINDER

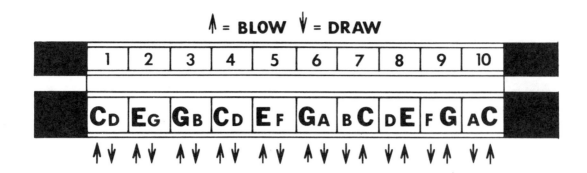

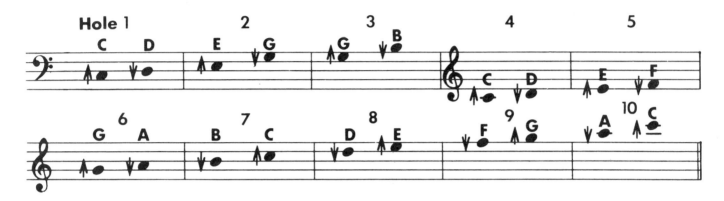

SHE'LL BE COMIN' ROUND THE MOUNTAIN

DIATONIC NOTE FINDER

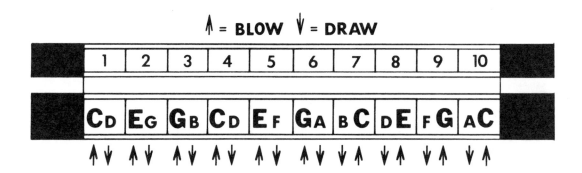

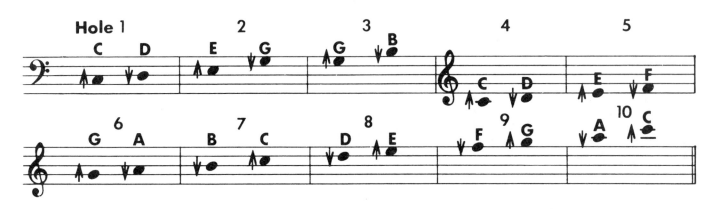

DIATONIC NOTE FINDER

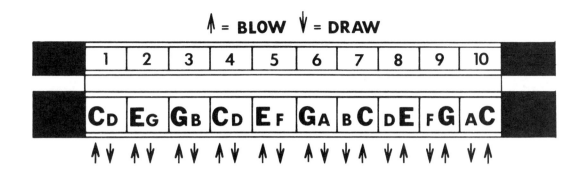

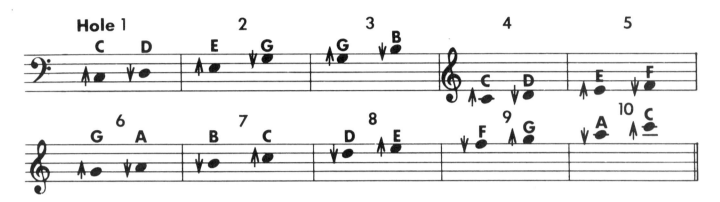

YELLOW ROSE OF TEXAS

24

DIATONIC NOTE FINDER

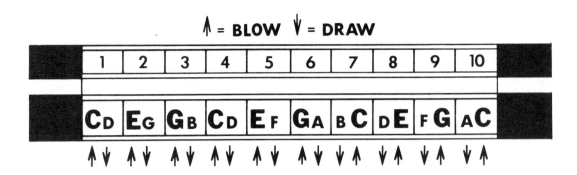

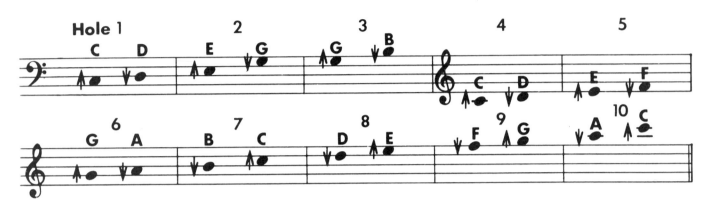

KUM BA YAH

DIATONIC NOTE FINDER

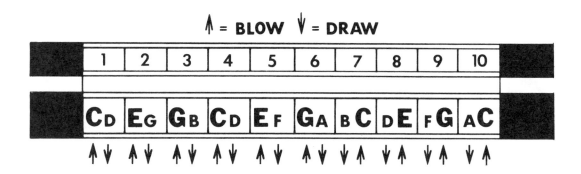

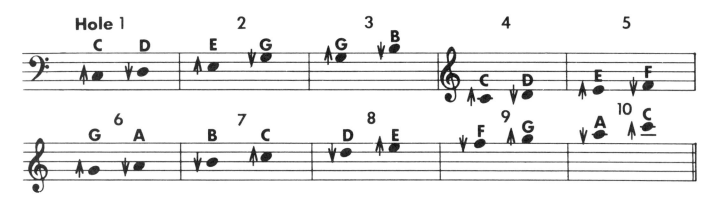

AMAZING GRACE

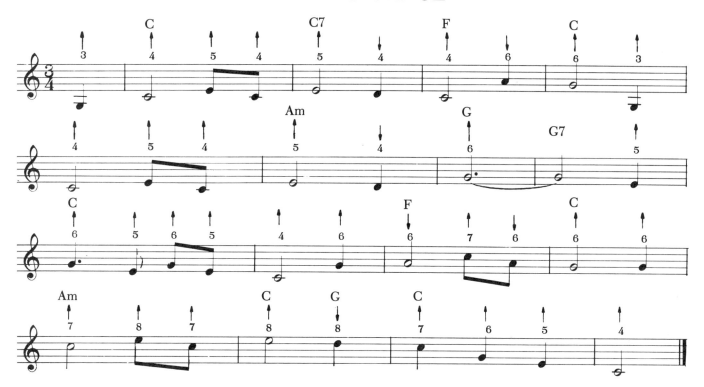

DIATONIC NOTE FINDER

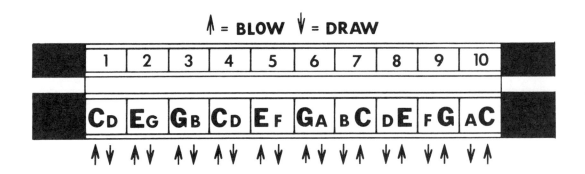

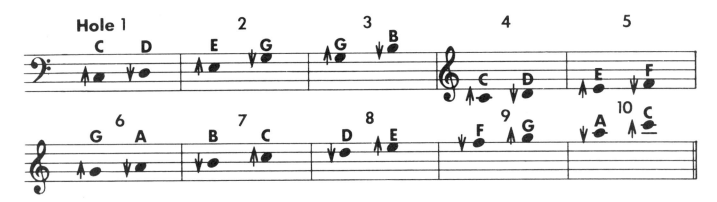

SWING LOW, SWEET CHARIOT

DIATONIC NOTE FINDER

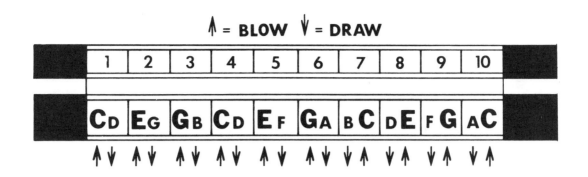

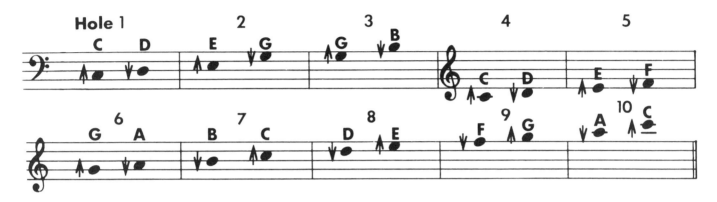

COME & GO WITH ME TO THAT LAND

DIATONIC NOTE FINDER

↑ = BLOW   ↓ = DRAW

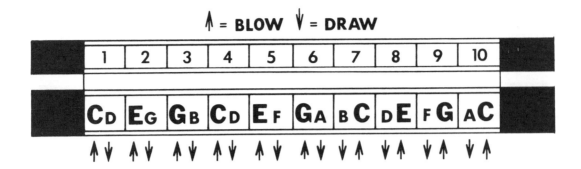

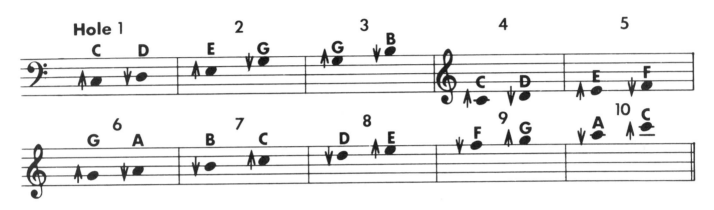

SHUFFLE RIFF BLUES

William Bay

DIATONIC NOTE FINDER

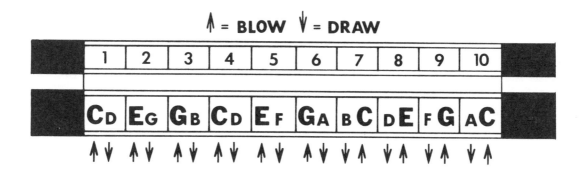

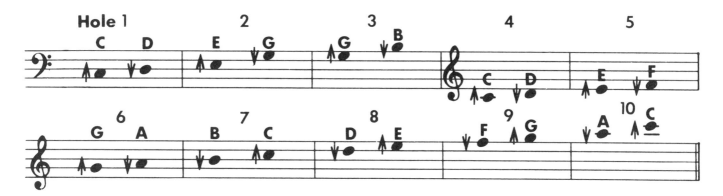

DRIVE RIFF BLUES

DIATONIC NOTE FINDER

↑ = BLOW ↓ = DRAW

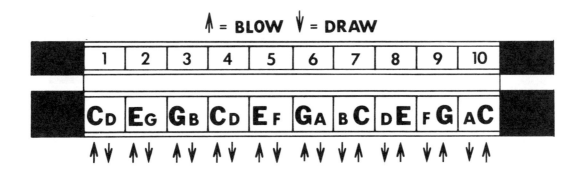

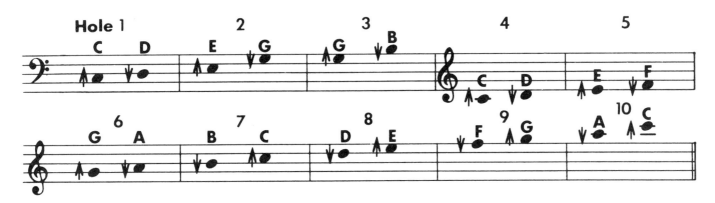

SLOW GROOVE BLUES

William Bay

Da   Da   Di   Di   Da   Da   Di   Di

DIATONIC NOTE FINDER

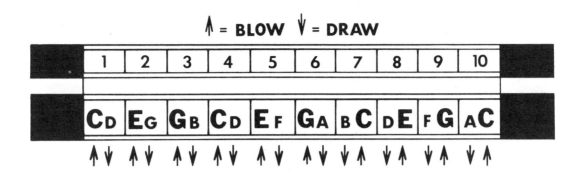

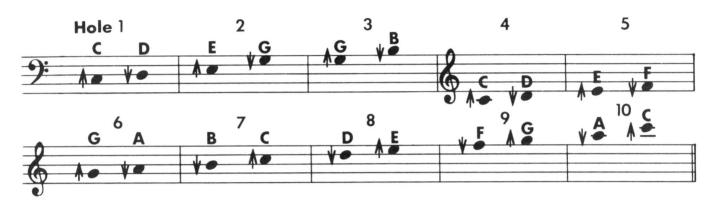

SLOW BLUES SOLO

William Bay

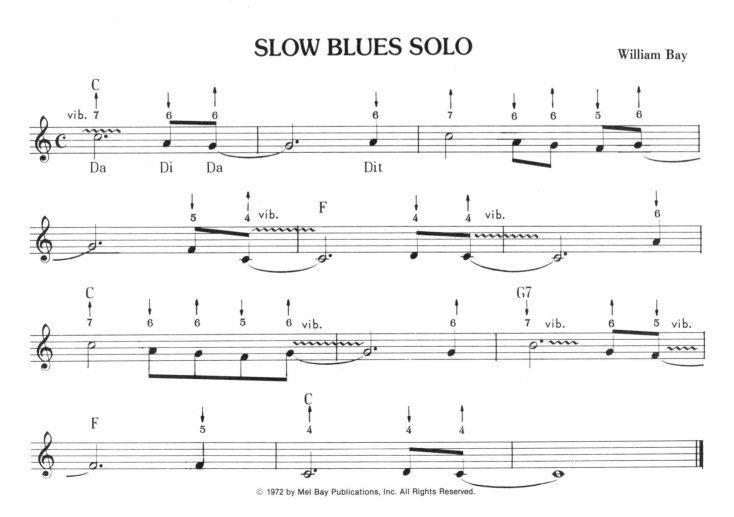

NATURE'S GREAT JOURNEYS

BISON
A WINTER JOURNEY

REBECCA HIRSCH
AND MARIA KORAN

MEDIA ENHANCED BOOKS
AV2 BY WEIGL
ADDED VALUE · AUDIO VISUAL

www.av2books.com

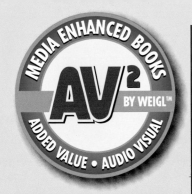

AV² provides enriched content that supplements and complements this book. Weigl's AV² books strive to create inspired learning and engage young minds in a total learning experience.

Your AV² Media Enhanced books come alive with...

Audio
Listen to sections of the book read aloud.

Key Words
Study vocabulary, and complete a matching word activity.

Video
Watch informative video clips.

Quizzes
Test your knowledge.

Go to **www.av2books.com,** and enter this book's unique code.

Embedded Weblinks
Gain additional information for research.

Slide Show
View images and captions, and prepare a presentation.

BOOK CODE

F 5 8 7 9 4 2

AV² by Weigl brings you media enhanced books that support active learning.

Try This!
Complete activities and hands-on experiments.

... and much, much more!

Published by AV² by Weigl
350 5th Avenue, 59th Floor
New York, NY 10118
Website: www.av2books.com

Library of Congress Cataloging-in-Publication Data

Names: Hirsch, Rebecca E. and Koran, Maria.
Title: Bison : a winter journey / Rebecca Hirsch and Maria Koran.
Description: New York, NY : AV2 by Weigl, [2017] | Series: Nature's great
 journeys | Includes bibliographical references and index.
Identifiers: LCCN 2016004420 (print) | LCCN 2016007035 (ebook) | ISBN
 9781489645111 (hard cover : alk. paper) | ISBN 9781489649898 (soft cover :
 alk. paper) | ISBN 9781489645128 (Multi-user ebk.)
Subjects: LCSH: Bison--Juvenile literature.
Classification: LCC QL737.U53 H546 2017 (print) | LCC QL737.U53 (ebook) | DDC
 599.64/3--dc23
LC record available at http://lccn.loc.gov/2016004420

Printed in the United States of America in Brainerd, Minnesota
1 2 3 4 5 6 7 8 9 0 20 19 18 17 16

072016
071416

Project Coordinator: Maria Koran   Art Director: Terry Paulhus

Contents

AMERICAN BISON

Millions of American bison once grazed across much of North America. They roamed over the grassy **prairies**, mountains, and open forests. Huge herds moved together. The animals' snorting and grunting filled the air. When startled or in danger, the herds ran. They kicked up thick clouds of dust. They caused the ground to tremble. The herds never stayed in one place for long. They were always on the move, searching for fresh food to eat.

The bison's lifetime journey is their migration. This is when an animal moves from one **habitat** to another. Migrations happen for many reasons. Some animals move to be in warmer weather where there is more food. There they can reproduce, or have their babies. And these migrations can be long distances. Or they can be short distances, such as from a **plateau** to its valley. Sometimes migrations include both short and long distances, such as the bison's search for food.

Bison live in groups called herds.

MIGRATION MAP

Wild bison live in small herds across the United States, Mexico, and Canada. The largest herd in the United States has more than 2,000 animals. This herd lives in Yellowstone National Park.

Yellowstone sits on a plateau, an area high above sea level. Yellowstone's bison migrate with the seasons. They have a **seasonal** migration. In summer, the bison graze over the high, grassy plateau. In fall, they migrate to the lower valleys. When winters are very cold, some bison migrate out of the park. In spring, they return to the plateau.

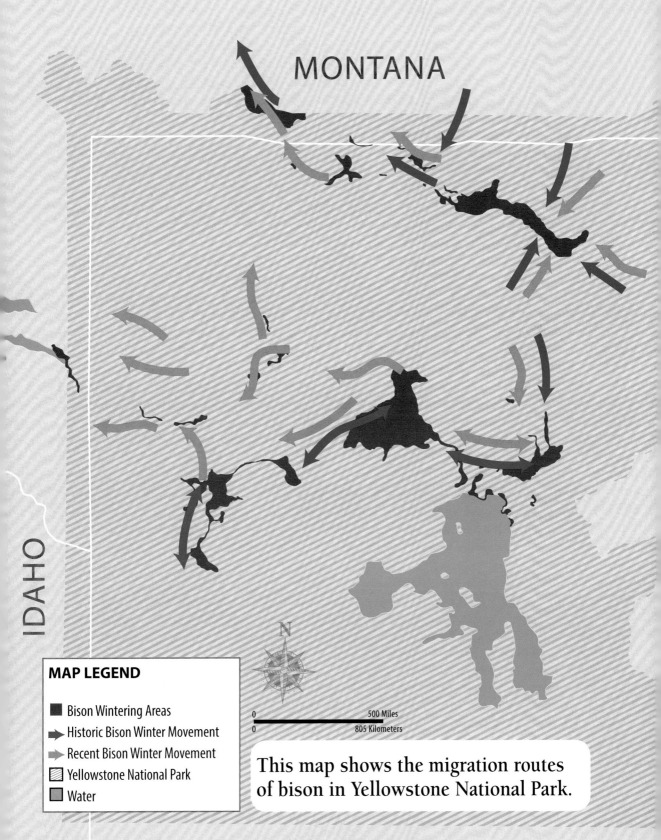

MONTANA

IDAHO

MAP LEGEND

■ Bison Wintering Areas
➤ Historic Bison Winter Movement
➤ Recent Bison Winter Movement
▨ Yellowstone National Park
■ Water

| 0 | 500 Miles |
| 0 | 805 Kilometers |

This map shows the migration routes of bison in Yellowstone National Park.

WYOMING

KINGS OF THE PRAIRIE

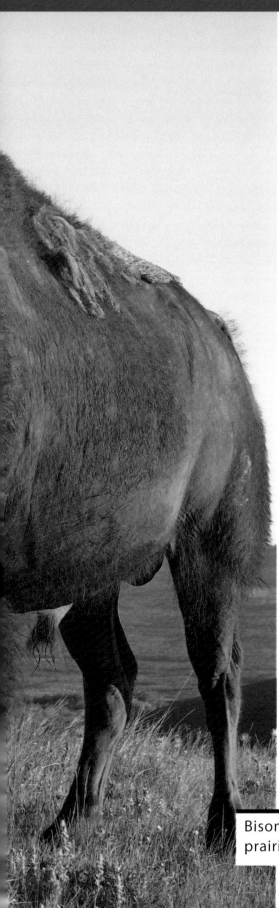

Bison are huge prairie animals.

Bison are the largest land animals in North America. The males, or bulls, stand about 6 feet (2 m) high at the shoulder. They can weigh more than 2,000 pounds (1,000 kg). That's as much as four large grizzly bears! The females, or cows, are smaller. They weigh more than 1,000 pounds (454 kg), though.

Bison have huge humps at the shoulders. Bison have thick, heavy fur. It protects them from the cold in winter and hot sun in summer. They have large heads topped with mops of dark hair. Their heads are crowned with sharp, curved horns.

Scientists call bison "American bison." But when white settlers first came to North America, they called bison "buffalo." American bison are different animals than buffalo, which live in Asia and Africa. But the name stuck. Most people in the United States call these animals buffalo.

HISTORIC MIGRATION

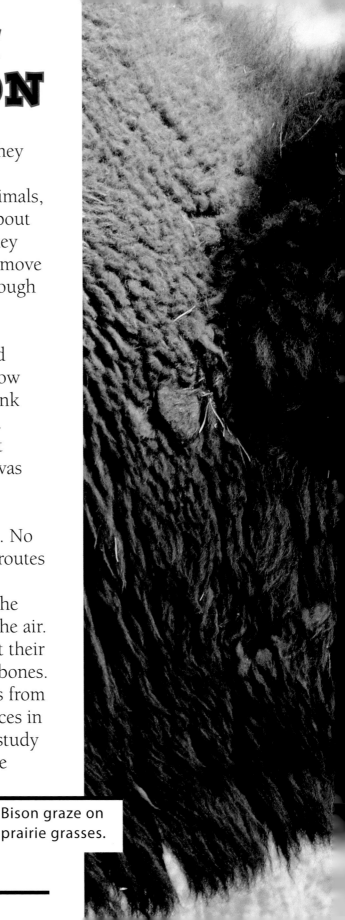

American bison are grazers. They feed on grasses, **sedges**, and shrubs. Because they are large animals, they eat a lot of grass. They eat about 30 pounds (14 kg) a day. After they eat all the grass in one area, they move on to find more grass. To find enough food to eat, bison herds migrate.

Giant herds of bison once roamed North America. No one knows how many bison there were. Many think there were once 30 to 60 million. These herds migrated throughout the year. They went where food was growing in each season.

These giant herds no longer exist. No one knows what their migration routes looked like. A few of their routes remain as paths worn deep into the soil. They can still be seen from the air. Scientists have also learned about their migration by studying old bison bones. As a bison grazes, it gets minerals from its food. These minerals leave traces in the bison's bones. Scientists can study the traces to learn how and where bison once lived.

Bison graze on prairie grasses.

Like their close relatives, cows, bison chew their food and swallow it. The food breaks down into smaller pieces in the stomach. Then the bison brings the food back up into their mouths again. They chew the food again and swallow it. This helps bison eat tough, chewy grasses.

BISON AND PRAIRIES

Many bison lived in the grasslands that once covered the middle of North America. These prairies went on in all directions. Prairies were the perfect place for animals that eat grass.

Many animals made prairies their home. **Predators** lived there, too. They included grizzly bears, wolves, and coyotes. But the bison was king. Vast herds of the large, shaggy animals once thundered across the prairie.

The prairie is an **ecosystem**. That is a place where all of the animals and plants live together. They depend on each other.

Bison help the prairie ecosystem in many ways. They dig up the soil with their sharp hooves. This pushes new seeds into the earth. It helps the prairie plants grow. Bison's grazing keeps the prairie grasses short. This makes the grasses grow even faster. The grazing also helps prairie dogs. They can watch for predators from the shorter grass.

Bison help other prairie animals, too. During the hot prairie summers, bison cool off by rolling on the ground. This makes dents in the ground called **wallows**. When rain comes, the wallows fill with water. The wallows turn into tiny ponds. Ducks and insects live in the ponds. Even the bison's droppings, called dung, are important. Bison dung puts **nutrients** in the soil. The rich soil is home to beetles and worms.

Many animals live in the prairies.

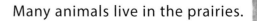

Hunting such a large, fast animal was not easy. Native Americans found a way, though. They hunted bison by driving the **stampedes** off cliffs. Later they hunted them from horseback using guns or bows and arrows.

BISON AND THE PLAINS INDIANS

For thousands of years, Native Americans lived in the prairies with the bison. The Plains Indians hunted bison and used every part of the animal. They ate bison meat. They used bison skin to make clothing and other things. They shaped the bones into tools. They used the rough tongue as a hairbrush. The dung was used as fuel for cooking.

The bison was important to the Plains Indians. They had deep respect for the animal. They honored the animals with songs and dances.

Snowshoes helped hunters get close to bison in winter. The bison could not move quickly in deep snow.

THE BISON DISAPPEARS

White settlers found millions and millions of bison when they moved to the prairies. But the settlers would almost cause the bison to disappear forever. The white settlers thought the bison were pests. They shot them in great numbers. Settlers thought they were unsafe for trains. When railroads were built across the prairies, bison stood on the tracks. Sometimes the animals pushed trains off the tracks. White hunters began shooting bison for their skins. The bison herds grew smaller and smaller.

In the late 1800s, few wild bison were left in the United States and Canada. People were afraid. They realized the bison could soon become **extinct**. This meant these animals could be lost forever.

Not only had the bison disappeared, but their prairie habitat had disappeared as well. Settlers had plowed the prairie. They destroyed the grasslands the bison needed. In the prairies, settlers grew fields of wheat, corn, and other crops.

Bison bones did not go to waste. They were used to make sugar, dishes, paint, and fertilizer.

A PLACE FOR BISON

People thought Yellowstone National Park could be the one place where bison could live. The new park was the first national park in the world. It was created in 1872 to help protect wildlife in the United States. One of the last remaining bison herds was discovered hidden in a valley of the park. But it was very small. It only had about 20 animals.

People decided to act. Bison were brought from zoos and ranches to Yellowstone. The bison were released. Slowly the herd grew. Today the Yellowstone herd is a great success. It is one of the largest herds of wild bison in North America. In Yellowstone, the herd still migrates during the seasons.

Yellowstone National Park is home to the largest wild bison herd in North America.

LIFE IN A HERD

A bison herd is made of four to 20 adult females and their calves. The females stay together for life. The males stay with the herd until they are about three years old. Then they leave. Males live alone. Or they group together in small herds with other males.

Living in a herd helps the bison stay safe. In a herd they can group together. If a wolf or grizzly bear comes too close, the cows form a circle around the calves. If a bull is in the herd, the bull stands on the outside. The cows stand behind the bull. The adults lower their heads and point their large horns out. The calves stay safe inside the circle.

Running is another way bison stay safe. Bison can run fast—faster than most horses. Bison can reach up to 40 miles (65 km) an hour. They can also turn quickly when running. When a bison sees something unusual, it runs. Soon the whole herd runs and the ground shakes. This is called a stampede. The predator often cannot catch even one animal.

Bison can hear very well. They can also detect odors from more than 1 mile (2 km) away.

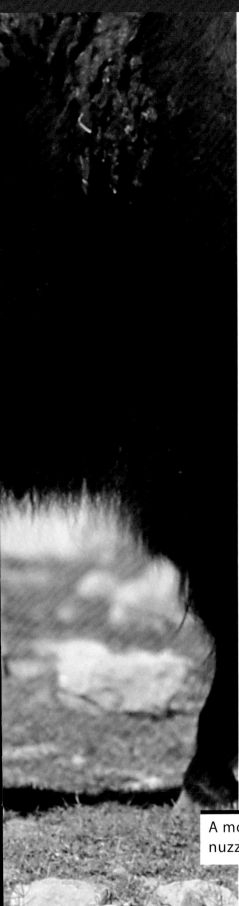

SPRING AND SUMMER

Life for a Yellowstone bison begins in spring. That is the season when the mother bison give birth to their young. Each cow licks her orange–colored calf clean. Then the calf takes its first wobbly steps. Within a few hours it can walk.

In just a few weeks the calf stops drinking its mother's milk. Then it joins the rest of the herd to graze. With the herd always on the move, the calf must keep up. It is in danger if it wanders from the herd.

A calf's first spring and summer is a very important time. The calf must gain weight and grow strong to survive the winter. It needs to gain about six times its weight before the snow comes. By its first birthday, a bison may weigh more than 400 pounds (181 kg).

In summer, males and females come together to mate. Males battle to see which is stronger. They butt heads and push until one gives way. The winner gets to choose a mate.

A mother bison nuzzles her calf.

WINTER IN YELLOWSTONE

Bison are built to survive the cold. Their thick winter coats and layers of fat keep them warm. They might wander close to one of the hot springs in the park. The springs give the bison extra warmth. When the cold wind blows, they turn to face the wind. They shake the snow off their shaggy backs. To push aside snow, they lower their heads and sweep them from side to side.

Bison can even find food in winter. They press their noses into the snow and smell deeply. They can smell grass through 3 feet (1 m) of snow. When they find some, they dig with their sharp hooves. They reach the grass under the snow.

Winters can be very cold. Temperatures stay below freezing during the day. It gets even colder at night. Snowfall can be heavy. Some spots in the park get as much as 25 feet (8 m) of snow in a winter. That is enough to bury a two–story house.

In the winter, many of the bison leave the high plateau. They go to the warmer valleys. But sometimes, the snow becomes so deep that bison cannot dig to the grasses. They must leave to find food. Otherwise, they could starve.

The oldest female leads the herd along worn trails and river valleys. She makes a path through the deep snow. The herd follows in a straight line.

To stay alive, the calves must stay close to the herd. If a young bison wanders off the path, it could get stuck in deep snow. If it falls into an icy river, the bison might drown. Winter migration is a dangerous time for a young bison.

Bison know how to survive cold winters.

If bison wander outside of Yellowstone, they can be killed.

THREATS TO BISON

Most winters, bison can find all the food they need inside Yellowstone. But sometimes the bison leave the park to find food. When Yellowstone's bison cross over the park's borders, they are in danger.

Inside Yellowstone, the bison are kept safe by law. People cannot hunt bison inside the park. But outside the park in Montana, bison can be shot and killed.

Why would someone shoot a bison? Some wild bison have a disease called **brucellosis**. This disease can also infect cattle. In pregnant cattle, the disease causes death of the calf. Ranchers fear the migrating bison will infect their cattle. They shoot and kill bison that wander too close to their ranches.

Bison can live up to 20 years in the wild.

SAVING THE BISON

Today the total number of bison in North America is about 200,000 to 250,000. Most live on ranches, where they are raised like cattle for meat. Ranch bison still look like their wild cousins, but they are different. Over time, ranchers have **domesticated** bison. They select only the most gentle animals to breed. Slowly the wildness in ranch bison has disappeared. Ranch bison do not fight or stampede. They spend all their lives on ranches. They also do not migrate.

Native American tribes are helping to restore wild bison. Today dozens of tribes have joined together to help. So far, the tribes have gathered herds that have almost 10,000 animals. Many tribes now have their own bison herds. And some still hunt the animals on horseback. They see the bison as an important part of Native American life.

Other wild herds, like the ones in Yellowstone, live on **reserves**. These **reserves** are found across the original land of bison. In these places, herds of wild bison still migrate like the bison that once filled the prairies.

Many bison now live on ranches and do not migrate.

QUIZ

1 What is a group of bison called?

A. A herd

2 How long can bison live in the wild?

A. Up to 20 years

3 How did Native Americans hunt herds of bison?

A. By driving the stampedes off cliffs

4 How much grass does a bison eat each day?

A. About 30 pounds (14 kg)

5 Who leads the herd along worn trails and river valleys in the winter?

A. The oldest female

6 Why do bison migrate?

A. To find enough food to eat

7 What parts of the bison did the Plains Indians use?

A. They used every part of the bison

8 Who almost caused the bison to become extinct?

A. White settlers on the prairies

9 How fast can bison run?

A. Up to 40 miles (65 km) an hour

10 What is brucellosis?

A. A disease in wild bison

KEY WORDS

brucellosis: Brucellosis is a disease that harms cattle and bison. Bison can pass brucellosis to cattle.

domesticated: A domesticated animal is one that is not wild and can live with or by people. Many bison are now domesticated.

ecosystem: An ecosystem is a community of plants and animals that depend on each other and the land. A prairie is an ecosystem.

extinct: A type of animal is extinct if it has died out. Bison almost became extinct.

habitat: A habitat is a place that has the food, water, and shelter an animal needs to survive. Bison move from one habitat to another.

nutrients: Nutrients are things that people, animals, and plants need to stay alive. Bison dung adds nutrients to the soil.

plateau: A plateau is an area of high, flat land. In the winter, bison move from the plateau to the valleys.

prairies: Prairies are large areas of grassy land with few or no trees. Prairies in the United States were once much bigger than they are today.

predators: Predators are animals that hunt and eat other animals. Predators live in the prairies.

reserves: Reserves are places that are set aside to keep animals and plants safe. Bison are safe on the reserves.

seasonal: Seasonal is something related to the seasons of the year. A seasonal migration is when animals move from one place to another with the seasons.

sedges: Sedges are plants that grow in wet ground. Bison eat sedges.

stampedes: Stampedes are when animals run wildly in one direction. Bison stampedes contain many animals.

wallows: Wallows are dents in the ground made by bison. Water collects in wallows made by bison.

INDEX

Log on to www.av2books.com

AV² by Weigl brings you media enhanced books that support active learning. Go to www.av2books.com, and enter the special code found on page 2 of this book. You will gain access to enriched and enhanced content that supplements and complements this book. Content includes video, audio, weblinks, quizzes, a slide show, and activities.

AV² Online Navigation

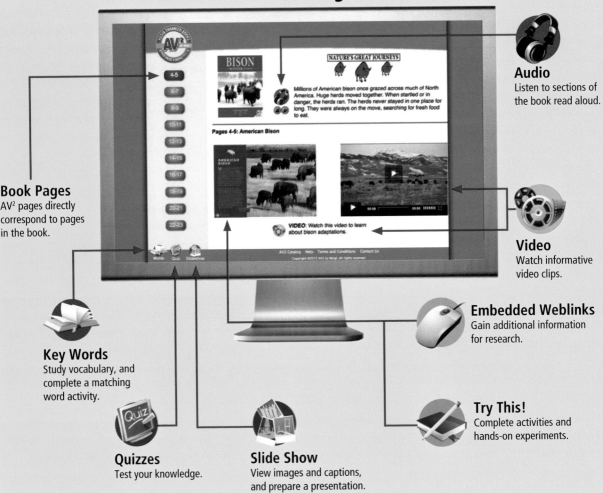

Audio
Listen to sections of the book read aloud.

Book Pages
AV² pages directly correspond to pages in the book.

Video
Watch informative video clips.

Embedded Weblinks
Gain additional information for research.

Key Words
Study vocabulary, and complete a matching word activity.

Try This!
Complete activities and hands-on experiments.

Quizzes
Test your knowledge.

Slide Show
View images and captions, and prepare a presentation.

AV² was built to bridge the gap between print and digital. We encourage you to tell us what you like and what you want to see in the future.

Sign up to be an AV² Ambassador at www.av2books.com/ambassador.

Due to the dynamic nature of the Internet, some of the URLs and activities provided as part of AV² by Weigl may have changed or ceased to exist. AV² by Weigl accepts no responsibility for any such changes. All media enhanced books are regularly monitored to update addresses and sites in a timely manner. Contact AV² by Weigl at 1-866-649-3445 or av2books@weigl.com with any questions, comments, or feedback.